CHI

Take Care of Your Eyes

By Don L. Curry

Consultant
Nanci R. Vargus, Ed.D.
Assistant Professor of Literacy
University of Indianapolis, Indianapolis, Indiana

Children's Press®
A Division of Scholastic Inc.
New York   Toronto   London   Auckland   Sydney
Mexico City   New Delhi   Hong Kong
Danbury, Connecticut

Designer: Herman Adler Design
Photo Researcher: Caroline Anderson
The photo on the cover shows a girl getting an eye exam.

Library of Congress Cataloging-in-Publication Data

Curry, Don L.
  Take care of your eyes / Don L. Curry.
    p. cm. — (Rookie read-about health)
  Includes index.
  ISBN 0-516-25874-5 (lib. bdg.)   0-516-27914-9 (pbk.)
  1. Eye—Care and hygiene—Juvenile literature. I. Title. II. Series.
  RE52.C875 2005
  617.7—dc22
                                      2004015302

CHILDREN'S PRESS, and ROOKIE READ-ABOUT®,
and associated logos are trademarks and or registered trademarks
of Scholastic Library Publishing. SCHOLASTIC and associated logos
are trademarks and or registered trademarks of Scholastic Inc.

1 2 3 4 5 6 7 8 9 10 R 14 13 12 11 10 09 08 07 06 05

What do you see in this picture?

4

What did you use to see those things?

You used your eyes! Your eyes are amazing. They help you see all the things you need to see.

You use your eyes to help you play. You use your eyes to help you draw pictures. You use your eyes to help you write, too.

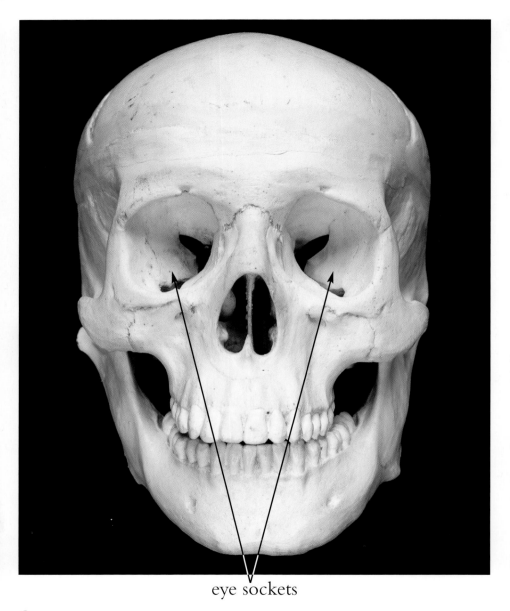

eye sockets

Your eyes sit in small holes in the front of your head. These holes are called eye sockets.

The hard bones of your head protect your eyes.

Your eye has different parts. Your iris is the colorful part of your eye. Your pupil is the black circle in the middle.

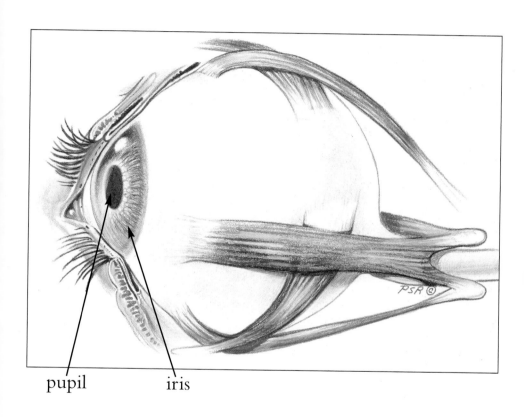

pupil   iris

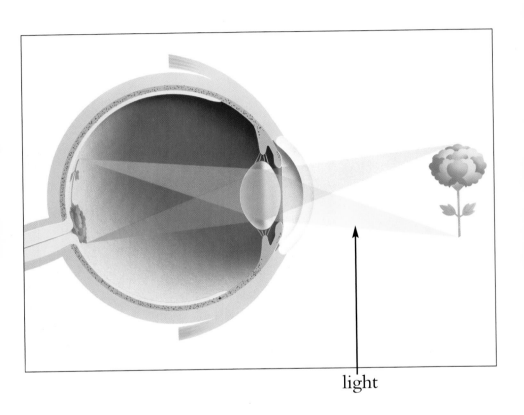

light

Your pupil opens to let in light. The light passes through your pupil until it reaches a nerve in the back of your eye.

The nerve sends messages to your brain. These messages tell your brain what you are seeing.

pupil

Your pupil opens wide
when it is dark.

Your pupil gets smaller in bright light. This protects your eyes from too much light.

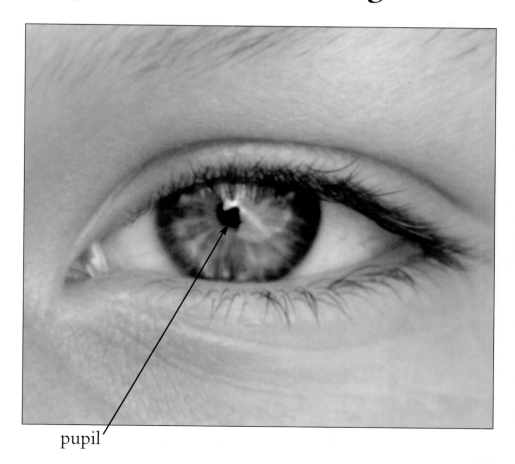

pupil

You should protect your eyes.

Never look directly at the Sun. Always wear sunglasses on a sunny day.

What else protects
your eyes?

Your eyelids do! They
keep your eyes clean
and moist.

eyebrow   eyelash

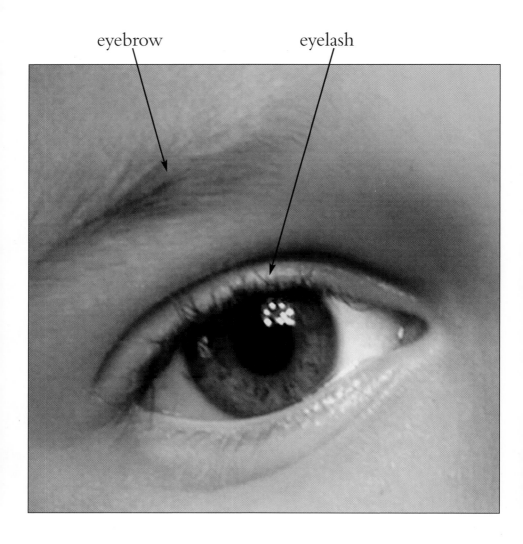

Your eyebrows and eyelashes help protect your eyes, too.

They help to keep out dust.

If something does get in your eyes, ask an adult for help.

Do not rub your eyes. You might hurt them.

Be sure to protect your eyes when you play sports.

These girls wear goggles when they swim.

These boys wear helmets to protect their faces.

An eye doctor can look
at your eyes.

The doctor may give
you glasses to help you
see better.

Take good care of
your eyes.

There is a lot to see in
the world!

29

Words You Know

eye doctor

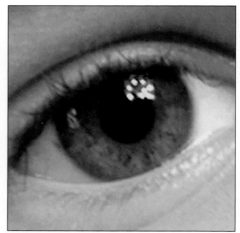

eyelashes

eyelids

goggles

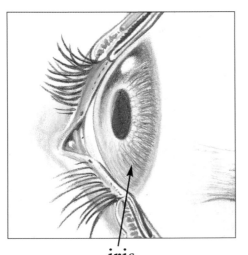

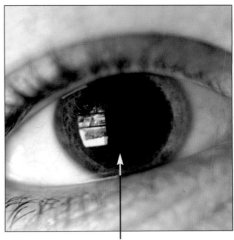

iris   pupil

sunglasses

Index

About the Author

Don L. Curry is a writer, editor, and consultant who lives and works in New York City. He has written more than 30 nonfiction books about science. The study of the human body is by far his favorite topic. When Don is not writing, he can be found reading in Central Park or riding his bike on the streets of "the greatest city on Earth."

Photo Credits

Photographs © 2005: Corbis Images: 24, 30 bottom right (George Contorakes), 29 (William Gottlieb), 23 (Rob Lewine); Photo Researchers, NY: 12 (Hans-Ulrich Osterwalder/SPL), 8 (Dennis Potokar), 11, 31 top left (Paul Singh-Roy); PhotoEdit: 19, 30 bottom left (Myrleen Ferguson Cate), 20, 30 top right (Lon C. Diehl), 25 (Robert W. Ginn), 26, 30 top left (Michael Newman), 3 (Nancy Sheehan), 14, 15, 16, 31 bottom, 31 top right (David Young-Wolff); Stock Boston: cover (Bob Daemmrich), 4, 7 (Lawrence Migdale).